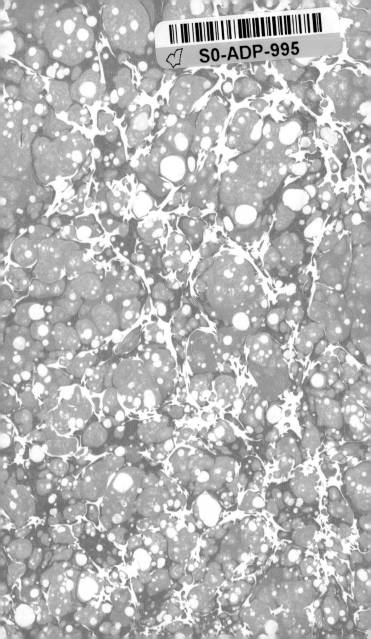

GREAT ENGLISH POETS

GREAT ENGLISH POETS

Lord Byron

Edited and with an introduction
by Peter Porter

 Clarkson N. Potter, Inc./Publishers NEW YORK

Published in the United States by Clarkson N. Potter, Inc.,
201 East 50th Street, New York, New York 10022
and distributed by Crown Publishers, Inc.
Published in Great Britain by Aurum Press Ltd.,
33 Museum Street, London WC1A 1LD

CLARKSON N. POTTER, POTTER, THE GREAT POETS,
and colophon are trademarks of Clarkson N. Potter, Inc.

Picture research by Juliet Brightmore

Manufactured in Hong Kong

Library of Congress Cataloging-in-Publication Data

Byron, George Byron, *Baron, 1788–1824*
(Poems. Selections)
Lord Byron. — edited by Peter Porter.
p. cm. — (Great poets series)
ISBN 0–517–57482–9: $8.95
I. Porter, Peter.   II. Title.   III. Series
PR4353.P67   1989
821/.7—dc20   89–15932
CIP

10   9   8   7   6   5   4   3   2   1
First American Edition

CONTENTS

INTRODUCTION

With Shakespeare, George Gordon, Lord Byron is the most celebrated English poet outside the English-speaking world, and one of the supreme literary figures within it. He established single-handed the special aura of Romanticism which excited whole generations of European poets, including such remarkable men as Gérard de Nerval, Pushkin and Lermontov. His narrative poems, *The Corsair* and *Parisina*, and his speculative plays, *Marino Faliero* and *The Two Foscari*, were turned into nineteenth-century Italian operas by Donizetti and Verdi, and even Goethe, already an old man when Byron was writing, felt the force of his influence.

Byron's death from fever at Missolonghi in 1824, at the head of an army he had raised and paid for himself, led directly to the liberation of Greece. Fired by his martyrdom, the British public forced a reluctant government to send a fleet against the Turks at the Battle of Navarino and so pave the way for Greek independence.

Byron's life was characteristically short in the manner of Romantic poets – thirty-six years against his friends Shelley's and Keats's twenty-nine and twenty-six respectively. But at his death he was the most famous poet in Europe and the most notorious sexual adventurer. While an undergraduate at Cambridge he kept a pet bear in the porter's lodge; on the Grand Tour he posed for his portrait in Albanian costume and swam the Hellespont, lived with brigands and visited seraglios. His liaisons with aristocratic beauties such as Lady Caroline Lamb and Lady Oxford kept his name before a fascinated public, and the scandal of his disputed divorce from an

heiress, Annabella Milbanke, whom he nicknamed 'the Princess of Parallelograms' for her reserved and scientific composure, destroyed his standing in English society. He left England for good in 1816 and wrote his greatest poetry in exile.

Yet the truly remarkable thing about Byron is his poetry – on the one hand, it is revolutionary in its romantic self-dramatization; on the other, it places him as the true inheritor of the Augustan precision and control of Alexander Pope. He wrote with wonderful fluency and his copious output ranges widely over many subjects and scenes, from picturesque travelogues of the Levant to house-parties in the depths of the English countryside. Byron was the worldliest of poets, yet he kept a freshness of utterance in everything he wrote. He was melancholy and ebullient at once, generous and bitter, a peer of the realm and a convinced democrat, his only consistency being his moral and physical courage.

Nowadays we see Byron as very different from his contemporaries' view of him as the supreme Romantic. Working from his best poems, *The Vision of Judgment, Beppo* and *Don Juan*, we esteem him as a pioneer of the conviction that 'light' or social verse may be as fully perceptive of the human condition as the solemn contemplation of Nature and Man practised by Wordsworth and his followers. But this revision must not be taken too far. Byron wrote a formidable body of poetry charged with that aura of doubt and exaggerated despair which is the hallmark of Romanticism. The fashionable image he created for himself made him the cynosure of Europe and gave us our adjective 'Byronic'. It is represented best today by *Childe Harold's Pilgrimage*. The publication of the first canto of this poem in 1812 made

Byron famous overnight. *Childe Harold* is constructed by the simplest and most effective means. Harold's European and Levantine travels form the background to the poem; Harold himself is just a peg for Byron to hang his observations on. The set-piece descriptions, however, are magnificent, as the stanzas devoted to Venice show.

The irony of Byron's long period of exile – 1816 to 1824, most of which he passed in Italy, at Venice, Ravenna, Pisa and Genoa – is the way in which it made him brood on his homeland, resulting in a magnificent set of letters back to friends in London and turning him increasingly to scenes from his English triumphs in the poems he wrote from 1818 onwards. These letters, which have been published in unexpurgated form only in the past decade, are perhaps the richest in all English literature. They paint the sharpest and most wide-ranging picture of the way people lived, netting the whole panorama realistically in words at once precise and evocative. The same realism leavened by humour became his chosen style in poetry. He borrowed the stanza known as *ottava rima* from Italian poetry and produced, in *Don Juan*, the most readable long poem in our language. At the end, Byron was writing verse as accurate, moving and witty as the prose he had always used in his letters.

It is a peculiarity of Byron's poetry that his finest work is to be found in his long poems. Extended passages from *Childe Harold* and *Don Juan* lie at the heart of his achievement, and I have, in consequence, chosen liberally from these for this brief selection of Byron's work. To help place each extract I have printed it under an explanatory heading of my own devising. Its source is given in a note at the end of the book.

Martial, Book 1, Epigram 1

He unto whom thou art so partial,
Oh, reader! is the well-known Martial,
The Epigrammatist: while living,
Give him the fame thou wouldst be giving;
So shall he hear, and feel, and know it –
    Post-obits rarely reach a poet.

Adrian's Address to His Soul When Dying

'Animula, vagula, blandula'

Ah! gentle, fleeting, wavering sprite,
Friend and associate of this clay!
    To what unknown region borne,
Wilt thou now wing thy distant flight?
No more with wonted humour gay,
    But pallid, cheerless, and forlorn.

From
CHILDE HAROLD'S PILGRIMAGE

Harold in Greece

And yet how lovely in thine age of woe,
Land of lost gods and godlike men! art thou!
Thy vales of ever-green, thy hills of snow
Proclaim thee Nature's varied favourite now:
Thy fanes, thy temples to thy surface bow,
Commingling slowly with heroic earth,
Broke by the share of every rustic plough:
So perish monuments of mortal birth,
So perish all in turn, save well-recorded Worth;

Save where some solitary column mourns
Above its prostrate brethren of the cave;
Save where Tritonia's airy shrine adorns
Colonna's cliff, and gleams along the wave;
Save o'er some warrior's half-forgotten grave,
Where the grey stones and unmolested grass
Ages, but not oblivion, feebly brave,
While strangers only not regardless pass,
Lingering like me, perchance, to gaze, and sigh 'Alas!'

Yet are thy skies as blue, thy crags as wild;
Sweet are thy groves, and verdant are thy fields,
Thine olive ripe as when Minerva smil'd,
And still his honied wealth Hymettus yields;
There the blithe bee his fragrant fortress builds,
The freeborn wanderer of thy mountain-air,
Apollo still thy long, long summer gilds,
Still in his beam Mendeli's marbles glare;
Art, Glory, Freedom fail, but Nature still is fair.

Where'er we tread 'tis haunted, holy ground;
No earth of thine is lost in vulgar mould,
But one vast realm of wonder spreads around,
All the Muse's tales seem truly old,
Till the sense aches with gazing to behold
The scenes our earliest dreams have dwelt upon:
Each hill and dale, each deepening glen and
    wold
Defies the power which crush'd thy temples
    gone:
Age shakes Athena's tower, but spares gray
    Marathon.

Harold's Lyric by the Rhine

The castled crag of Drachenfels
Frowns o'er the wide and winding Rhine,
Whose breast of waters broadly swells
Between the banks which bear the vine,
And hills all rich with blossomed trees,
And fields which promise corn and wine,
And scattered cities crowning these,
Whose far white walls along them shine,
Have strewed a scene, which I should see
With double joy wert *thou* with me!

And peasant girls, with deep blue eyes,
And hands which offer early flowers,
Walk smiling o'er this paradise;
Above, the frequent feudal towers
Through green leaves lift their walls of grey,
And many a rock which steeply lours,
And noble arch in proud decay,
Look o'er this vale of vintage-bowers;
But one thing want these banks of Rhine, –
Thy gentle hand to clasp in mine!

I send the lilies given to me;
Though long before thy hand they touch,
I know that they must withered be,
But yet reject them not as such;
For I have cherish'd them as dear,
Because they yet may meet thine eye,
And guide thy soul to mine even here,
When thou behold'st them droopng nigh,
And knowst them gathered by the Rhine,
And offered from my heart to thine!

The river nobly foams and flows,
The charm of this enchanted ground,
And all its thousand turns disclose
Some fresher beauty varying round;
The haughtiest breast its wish might bound
Through life to dwell delighted here;
Nor could on earth a spot be found
To nature and to me so dear,
Could thy dear eyes in following mine
Still sweeten more these banks of Rhine!

Harold Alone

I have not loved the world, nor the world me;
I have not flattered its rank breath, nor bow'd
To its idolatries a patient knee, –
Nor coin'd my cheek to smiles, – nor cried aloud
In worship of an echo; in the crowd
They could not deem me one of such; I stood
Among them, but not of them; in a shroud
Of thoughts which were not their thoughts, and
    still could,
Had I not filed my mind, which thus itself subdued.

I have not loved the world, nor the world me, –
But let us part fair foes; I do believe,
Though I have found them not, that there may
    be
Words which are things, – hopes which will not
    deceive,
And virtues which are merciful, nor weave
Snares for the failing: I would also deem
O'er others' griefs that some sincerely grieve;
That two, or one, are almost what they seem, –
That goodness is no name, and happiness no
    dream.

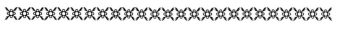

Harold in Venice

I stood in Venice, on the Bridge of Sighs;
A palace and a prison on each hand:
I saw from out the wave her structures rise
As from the stroke of the enchanter's wand:
A thousand years their cloudy wings expand
Around me, and a dying Glory smiles
O'er the far times, when many a subject land
Look'd to the winged Lion's marble piles,
Where Venice sate in state, thron'd on her
        hundred isles!

She looks a sea Cybele, fresh from ocean,
Rising with her tiara of proud towers
At airy distance, with majestic motion,
A ruler of the waters and their powers:
And such she was; – her daughters had their
        dowers
From spoils of nations, and the exhaustless East
Pour'd in her lap all gems in sparkling showers.
In purple was she robed, and of her feast
Monarchs partook, and deem'd their dignity
        increas'd.

In Venice Tasso's echoes are no more,
And silent rows the songless gondolier;
Her palaces are crumbling to the shore,
And music meets not always now the ear:
Those days are gone – but Beauty still is here.
States fall, arts fade – but Nature doth not die,
Nor yet forget how Venice once was dear,
The pleasant place of all festivity,
The revel of the earth, the masque of Italy!

But unto us she hath a spell beyond
Her name in story, and her long array
Of mighty shadows, whose dim forms despond
Above the dogeless city's vanish'd sway;
Ours is a trophy which will not decay
With the Rialto; Shylock and the Moor,
And Pierre, can not be swept or worn away –
The keystones of the arch! though all were o'er,
For us repeopled were the solitary shore.

Before St Mark still glow his steeds of brass,
Their gilded collars glittering in the sun;
But is not Doria's menace come to pass?
Are they *not bridled?* – Venice, lost and won,
Her thirteen hundred years of freedom done,
Sinks, like a sea-weed, into whence she rose!
Better be whelm'd beneath the waves, and shun,
Even in destruction's depth, her foreign foes,
From whom submission wrings an infamous repose.

Statues of glass – all shiver'd – the long file
Of her dead Doges are declin'd to dust;
But where they dwelt, the vast and sumptuous
pile
Bespeaks the pageant of their splendid trust;
Their sceptre broken, and their sword in rust,
Have yielded to the stranger: empty halls,
Thin streets, and foreign aspects, such as must
Too oft remind her who and what enthrals,
Have flung a desolate cloud o'er Venice' lovely
walls.

Harold's Philosophy

From mighty wrongs to petty perfidy
Have I not seen what human things could do?
From the loud roar of foaming calumny
To the small whisper of the as paltry few,
And subtler venom of the reptile crew,
The Janus glance of whose significant eye,
Learning to lie with silence, would *seem* true,
And without utterance, save the shrug or sigh,
Deal round to happy fools its speechless obloquy.

But I have lived, and have not lived in vain:
My mind may lose its force, my blood its fire,
And my frame perish even in conquering pain;
But there is that within me which shall tire
Torture and Time, and breathe when I expire;
Something unearthly, which they deem not of,
Like the remembered tone of a mute lyre,
Shall on their softened spirits sink, and move
In hearts all rocky now the late remorse of love.

The seal is set. – Now welcome, thou dread power!
Nameless, yet thus omnipotent, which here
Walk'st in the shadow of the midnight hour
With a deep awe, yet all distinct from fear;
Thy haunts are ever where the dead walls rear
Their ivy mantles, and the solemn scene
Derives from thee a sense so deep and clear
That we become a part of what has been,
And grow unto the spot, all-seeing but unseen.

She Walks in Beauty

She walks in beauty, like the night
    Of cloudless climes and starry skies;
And all that's best of dark and bright
    Meet in her aspect and her eyes:
Thus mellow'd to that tender light
    Which heaven to gaudy day denies.

One shade the more, one ray the less,
    Had half impair'd the nameless grace
Which waves in every raven tress,
    Or softly lightens o'er her face;
Where thoughts serenely sweet express
    How pure, how dear their dwelling place.

And on that cheek, and o'er that brow,
    So soft, so calm, yet eloquent,
The smiles that win, the tints that glow,
    But tell of days in goodness spent,
A mind at peace with all below,
    A heart whose love is innocent!

So, We'll Go No More A Roving

So, we'll go no more a roving
  So late into the night,
Though the heart be still as loving,
  And the moon be still as bright.

For the sword outwears its sheath,
  And the soul wears out the breast,
And the heart must pause to breathe,
  And love itself have rest.

Though the night was made for loving,
  And the day returns too soon,
Yet we'll go no more a roving
  By the light of the moon.

From THE ISLAND

Here, in this grotto of the wave-worn shore,
They passed the tropic's red meridian o'er;
Nor long the hours – they never paused o'er time,
Unbroken by the clock's funereal chime,
Which deals the daily pittance of our span,
And points and mocks with iron laugh at man.
What deemed they of the future or the past?
The present, like a tyrant, held them fast:
Their hour-glass was the sea-sand, and the tide,
Like her smooth billow, saw their moments glide;
Their clock the sun, in his unbounded tower;
They reckoned not, whose day was but an hour;
The nightingale, their only vesper-bell,
Sung sweetly to the rose the day's farewell;
The broad sun set, but not with lingering sweep,
As in the north he mellows o'er the deep;
But fiery, full, and fierce, as if he left
The world for ever, earth of light bereft,
Plunged with red forehead down along the wave,
As dives a hero headlong to his grave.
Then rose they, looking first along the skies,
And then for light into each other's eyes,
Wondering that summer showed so brief a sun,
And asking if indeed the day were done.

When We Two Parted

When we two parted
    In silence and tears
Half broken-hearted
    To sever for years,
Pale grew thy cheek and cold,
    Colder thy kiss;
Truly that hour foretold
    Sorrow to this.

The dew of the morning
    Sunk chill on my brow –
It felt like the warning
    Of what I feel now.
Thy vows are all broken,
    And light is thy fame;
I hear thy name spoken,
    And share in its shame.

They name thee before me,
    A knell to mine ear;
A shudder comes o'er me –
    Why wert thou so dear?
They know not I knew thee,
    Who knew thee too well: –
Long, long shall I rue thee,
    Too deeply to tell.

In secret we met –
    In silence I grieve,
That thy heart could forget,
    Thy spirit deceive.
If I should meet thee
    After long years,
How should I greet thee! –
    With silence and tears.

From THE VISION OF JUDGMENT

On Robert Southey

He said – (I only give the heads) – he said,
　He meant no harm in scribbling; 'twas his way
Upon all topics; 'twas, besides, his bread,
　Of which he butter'd both sides; 'twould delay
Too long the assembly (he was pleased to dread)
　And take up rather more time than a day,
To name his works – he would but cite a few –
Wat Tyler – Rhymes on Blenheim – Waterloo.

He had written praises of a regicide;
　He had written praises of all kings whatever,
He had written for republics far and wide,
　And then against them bitterer than ever,
For pantisocracy he once had cried
　Aloud, a scheme less moral than 'twas clever;
Then grew a hearty antijacobin –
Had turn'd his coat – and would have turn'd his skin.

He had sung against all battles, and again
　In their high praise and glory: he had call'd
Reviewing 'the ungentle craft,' and then
　Become as base a critic as ere crawl'd –
Fed, paid, and pamper'd by the very men
　By whom his muse and morals had been maul'd:
He had written much blank verse, and blanker prose,
And more of both than any body knows.

From BEPPO

On Italy and England

With all its sinful doings, I must say,
   That Italy's a pleasant place to me,
Who love to see the Sun shine every day,
   And vines (not nail'd to walls) from tree to tree
Festoon'd, much like the back scene of a play,
   Or melodrame, which people flock to see,
When the first act is ended by a dance
In vineyards copied from the south of France.

I love the language, that soft bastard Latin,
   Which melts like kisses from a female mouth,
And sounds as if it should be writ on satin,
   With syllables which breathe of the sweet South,
And gentle liquids gliding all so pat in,
   That not a single accent seems uncouth,
Like our harsh northern whistling, grunting guttural,
Which we're oblig'd to hiss, and spit, and sputter all.

I like the women too (forgive my folly),
   From the rich peasant-cheek of ruddy bronze,
And large black eyes that flash on you a volley
   Of rays that say a thousand things at once,
To the high dama's brow, more melancholy,
   But clear, and with a wild and liquid glance,
Heart on her lips, and soul within her eyes,
Soft as her clime, and sunny as her skies.

'England! with all thy faults I love thee still,'
    I said at Calais, and have not forgot it;
I like to speak and lucubrate my fill;
    I like the government (but that is not it);
I like the freedom of the press and quill;
    I like the Habeas Corpus (when we've got it);
I like a parliamentary debate,
Particularly when 'tis not too late;

I like the taxes, when they're not too many;
    I like a sea-coal fire, when not too dear;
I like a beef-steak, too, as well as any;
    Have no objection to a pot of beer;
I like the weather, when it is not rainy,
    That is, I like two months of every year,
And so God save the Regent, Church, and King!
Which means that I like all and everything.

Our standing army, and disbanded seamen,
    Poor's rate, Reform, my own, the nation's debt,
Our little riots just to show we are free men,
    Our trifling bankruptcies in the Gazette,
Our cloudy climate and our chilly women,
    All these I can forgive, and those forget,
And greatly venerate our recent glories,
And wish they were not owing to the Tories.

From DON JUAN

Fragment on the back of
the Ms. of Canto 1

I would to heaven that I were so much clay,
    As I am blood, bone, marrow, passion, feeling –
Because at least the past were passed away
    And for the future – (but I write this reeling,
Having got drunk exceedingly today,
    So that I seem to stand upon the ceiling)
I say – the future is a serious matter –
And so – for God's sake – hock and soda-water!

Comparative Morality

'Tis a sad thing, I cannot choose but say,
 And all the fault of that indecent sun,
Who cannot leave alone our helpless clay,
 But will keep baking, broiling, burning on,
That howsoever people fast and pray
 The flesh is frail, and so the soul undone:
What men call gallantry, and gods adultery,
Is much more common where the climate's sultry.

Happy the nations of the moral north!
 Where all is virtue, and the winter season
Sends sin, without a rag on, shivering forth;
 ('Twas snow that brought St Anthony to
  reason);
Where juries cast up what a wife is worth
 By laying whate'er sum, in mulct, they please on
The lover, who must pay a handsome price,
Because it is a marketable vice.

First Love

'Tis sweet to win, no matter how, one's laurels
    By blood or ink; 'tis sweet to put an end
To strife; 'tis sometimes sweet to have our quarrels,
    Particularly with a tiresome friend;
Sweet is old wine in bottles, ale in barrels;
    Dear is the helpless creature we defend
Against the world; and dear the schoolboy spot
We ne'er forget, though there we are forgot.

But sweeter still than this, than these, than all,
    Is first and passionate love – it stands alone,
Like Adam's recollection of his fall;
    The tree of knowledge has been pluck'd –
        all's known –
And life yields nothing further to recall
    Worthy of this ambrosial sin, so shown,
No doubt in fable, as the unforgiven
Fire which Prometheus filch'd for us from heaven.

Poetical Commandments

If ever I should condescend to prose,
    I'll write poetical commandments, which
Shall supersede beyond all doubt all those
    That went before; in these I shall enrich
My text with many things that no one knows,
    And carry precept to the highest pitch:
I'll call the work 'Longinus o'er a Bottle,
Or, Every Poet his *own* Aristotle'.

Thou shalt believe in Milton, Dryden, Pope;
    Thou shalt not set up Wordsworth, Coleridge,
        Southey;
Because the first is crazed beyond all hope,
    The second drunk, the third so quaint and
        mouthey:
With Crabbe it may be difficult to cope,
    And Campbell's Hippocrene is somewhat
        drouthy:
Thou shalt not steal from Samuel Rogers, nor
Commit – flirtation with the muse of Moore.

Haidée's Island and a Hangover

It was a wild and breaker-beaten coast,
  With cliffs above, and a broad sandy shore,
Guarded by shoals and rocks as by an host,
  With here and there a creek, whose aspect wore
A better welcome to the tempest-tost;
  And rarely ceased the haughty billow's roar,
Save on the dead long summer days, which make
The outstretch'd ocean glitter like a lake.

And the small ripple spilt upon the beach
  Scarcely o'erpass'd the cream of your
      champaigne,
When o'er the brim the sparkling bumpers reach,
  That spring-dew of the spirit! the heart's rain!
Few things surpass old wine; and they may preach
  Who please, – the more because they preach in
      vain, –
Let us have wine and woman, mirth and laughter,
Sermons and soda water the day after.

Juan and Haidée in Love

They look'd up to the sky, whose floating glow
    Spread like a rosy ocean, vast and bright;
They gazed upon the glittering sea below,
    Whence the broad moon rose circling into sight;
They heard the wave's splash, and the wind so low,
    And saw each other's dark eyes darting light
Into each other – and, beholding this,
Their lips drew near, and clung into a kiss;

A long, long kiss, a kiss of youth, and love,
    And beauty, all concentrating like rays
Into one focus, kindled from above;
    Such kisses as belong to early days,
Where heart, and soul, and sense, in concert
      move,
    And the blood's lava, and the pulse a blaze,
Each kiss a heart-quake, – for a kiss's strength,
I think, it must be reckon'd by its length.

They were alone, but not alone as they
    Who shut in chambers think it loneliness;
The silent ocean, and the starlight bay,
    The twilight glow, which momently grew less,
The voiceless sands, and dropping caves, that lay
    Around them, made them to each other press,
As if there were no life beneath the sky
Save theirs, and that their life could never die.

They feared no eyes nor ears on that lone beach,
    They felt no terrors from the night; they were
All in all to each other; though their speech
    Was broken words, they *thought* a language
        there, –
And all the burning tongues the passions teach
    Found in one sigh the best interpreter
Of nature's oracle – first love, – that all
Which Eve has left her daughters since her fall.

Alas! they were so young, so beautiful,
    So lonely, loving, helpless, and the hour
Was that in which the heart is always full
    And, having o'er itself no further power,
Prompts deeds eternity can not annul,
    But pays off moments in an endless shower
Of hell-fire – all prepared for people giving
Pleasure or pain to one another living.

They look upon each other, and their eyes
    Gleam in the moonlight; and her white arm
        clasps
Round Juan's head, and his around her lies
    Half buried in the tresses which it grasps;
She sits upon his knee, and drinks his sighs,
    He hers, until they end in broken gasps;
And thus they form a group that's quite antique,
Half naked, loving, natural, and Greek.

Haidée's Death

Thus lived – thus died she; never more on her
　Shall sorrow light, or shame. She was not made
Through years or moons the inner weight to bear,
　Which colder hearts endure till they are laid
By age in earth; her days and pleasure were
　Brief, but delightful – such as had not staid
Long with her destiny; but she sleeps well
By the sea shore, whereon she loved to dwell.

That isle is now all desolate and bare,
　Its dwellings down, its tenants past away;
None but her own and father's grave is there,
　And nothing outward tells of human clay;
Ye could not know where lies a thing so fair,
　No stone is there to show, no tongue to say
What was; no dirge, except the hollow sea's,
Mourns o'er the beauty of the Cyclades.

The Taking of Ismail and the Horrors of War

The town was taken – whether he might yield
  Himself or bastion, little mattered now;
His stubborn valour was no future shield.
  Ismail's no more! The crescent's silver bow
Sunk, and the crimson cross glared o'er the field,
  But red with no *redeeming* gore: the glow
Of burning streets, like moonlight on the water,
Was imaged back in blood, the sea of slaughter.

All that the mind would shrink from of excesses;
  All that the body perpetrates of bad;
All that we read, hear, dream, of man's distresses;
  All that the Devil would do if run stark mad;
All that defies the worst which pen expresses;
  All by which Hell is peopled, or as sad
As Hell – mere mortals who their power abuse, –
Was here (as heretofore and since) let loose.

If here and there some transient trait of pity
  Was shown, and some more noble heart broke
      through
Its bloody bond, and saved perhaps some pretty
  Child, or an aged, helpless man or two –
What's this in one annihilated city,
  Where thousand loves, and ties, and duties
      grew?
Cockneys of London! Muscadins of Paris!
Just ponder what a pious pastime war is.

The Duke of Wellington

Oh, Wellington! (or 'Vilainton' – for Fame
    Sounds the heroic syllables both ways;
France could not even conquer your great name,
    But punned it down to this facetious phrase –
Beating or beaten she will laugh the same) –
    You have obtained great pensions and much
        praise;
Glory like yours should any dare gainsay,
Humanity would rise, and thunder 'Nay!'

I don't think that you used Kinnaird quite well
    In Marinêt's affair – in fact 'twas shabby,
And like some other things won't do to tell
    Upon your tomb in Westminster's old abbey.
Upon the rest 'tis not worth while to dwell,
    Such tales being for the tea hours of some tabby;
But though your years as *man* tend fast to zero,
In fact your Grace is still but a *young Hero*.

Though Britain owes (and pays you too) so much,
    Yet Europe doubtless owes you greatly more:
You have repaired Legitimacy's crutch, –
    A prop not quite so certain as before:
The Spanish, and the French, as well as Dutch,
    Have seen, and felt, how strongly you *restore*;
And Waterloo has made the world your debtor –
(I wish your bards would sing it rather better).

You are 'the best of cut-throats:' – do not start;
  The phrase is Shakespeare's, and not misapplied: –
War's a brain-spattering, windpipe-slitting art,
  Unless her cause by Right be sanctified.
If you have acted *once* a generous part,
  The World, not the World's masters, will
    decide,
And I shall be delighted to learn who,
Save you and yours, have gained by Waterloo?

I am no flatterer – you've supped full of flattery:
  They say you like it too – 'tis no great wonder:
He whose whole life has been assault and battery,
  At last may get a little tired of thunder;
And swallowing eulogy much more than satire, he
  May like being praised for every lucky blunder,
Called 'Saviour of the Nations' – not yet saved,
And Europe's Liberator – still enslaved.

I've done. Now go and dine from off the plate
  Presented by the Prince of the Brazils,
And send the sentinel before your gate
  A slice or two from your luxurious meals:
He fought, but has not fed so well of late.
  Some hunger too they say the people feels: –
There is no doubt that you deserve your ration,
But pray give back a little to the nation.

The Prospect of London

A mighty mass of brick, and smoke, and shipping,
   Dirty and dusky, but as wide as eye
Could reach, with here and there a sail just
      skipping
   In sight, then lost amidst the forestry
Of masts; a wilderness of steeples peeping
   On tiptoe, through their sea-coal canopy;
A huge, dun cupola, like a foolscap crown
On a fool's head – and there is London Town!

But Juan saw not this: each wreath of smoke
   Appeared to him but as the magic vapour
Of some alchymic furnace, from whence broke
   The wealth of worlds (a wealth of tax and
      paper):
The gloomy clouds, which o'er it as a yoke
   Are bowed, and put the sun out like a taper,
Were nothing but the natural atmosphere,
Extremely wholesome, though but rarely clear.

Juan on Shooter's Hill

Don Juan had got out on Shooter's Hill;
　　Sunset the time, the place the same declivity
Which looks along that vale of good and ill
　　Where London streets ferment in full activity;
While every thing around was calm and still,
　　Except the creak of wheels, which on their pivot he
Heard, – and that bee-like, bubbling, busy hum
Of cities, that boil over with their scum: –

I say, Don Juan, wrapt in contemplation,
　　Walked on behind his carriage, o'er the summit,
And lost in wonder of so great a nation,
　　Gave way to't, since he could not overcome it.
'And here,' he cried, 'is Freedom's chosen station;
　　Here peals the people's voice, nor can entomb it
Racks, prisons, inquisitions; resurrection
Awaits it, each new meeting or election.

'Here are chaste wives, pure lives; here people pay
　　But what they please; and if that things be dear,
'Tis only that they love to throw away
　　Their cash, to show how much they have a year.
Here laws are all inviolate; none lay
　　Traps for the traveller, every highway's clear:
Here' – he was interrupted by a knife,
With, 'Damn your eyes! your money or your life!'

These freeborn sounds proceeded from four pads,
    In ambush laid, who had perceived him loiter
Behind his carriage; and, like handy lads,
    Had seized the lucky hour to reconnoitre,
In which the heedless gentleman who gads
    Upon the road, unless he prove a fighter,
May find himself within that isle of riches
Exposed to lose his life as well as breeches.

Juan, who did not understand a word
    Of English, save their shibboleth, 'God damn!'
And even that he had so rarely heard,
    He sometimes thought 'twas only their 'Salām,'
Or 'God be with you!' – and 'tis not absurd
    To think so; for half English as I am
(To my misfortune) never can I say
I heard them wish 'God with you,' save that way; –

Juan yet quickly understood their gesture,
    · And being somewhat choleric and sudden,
Drew forth a pocket-pistol from his vesture,
    And fired it into one assailant's pudding –
Who fell as rolls an ox o'er in his pasture,
    And roared out, as he writhed his native mud in,
Unto his nearest follower or henchman,
'Oh Jack! I'm floored by that 'ere bloody
        Frenchman!'

Newstead Abbey Recalled

The mansion's self was vast and venerable,
  With more of the monastic than has been
Elsewhere preserved: the cloisters still were stable,
  The cells too and refectory, I ween:
An exquisite small chapel had been able,
  Still unimpair'd, to decorate the scene;
The rest had been reform'd, replaced, or sunk,
And spoke more of the baron than the monk.

Huge halls, long galleries, spacious chambers,
    join'd
  By no quite lawful marriage of the Arts,
Might shock a Connoisseur; but when combined,
  Form'd a whole which, irregular in parts,
Yet left a grand impression on the mind,
  At least of those whose eyes are in their hearts.
We gaze upon a Giant for his stature,
Nor judge at first if all be true to Nature.

Steel Barons, molten the next generation
  To silken rows of gay and garter'd Earls,
Glanced from the walls in goodly preservation;
  And Lady Marys blooming into girls,
With fair long locks, had also kept their station:
  And Countesses mature in robes and pearls:
Also some beauties of Sir Peter Lely,
Whose drapery hints we may admire them freely.

Judges in very formidable ermine
   Were there, with brows that did not much invite
The accused to think their Lordships would
     determine
   His cause by leaning much from might to right:
Bishops, who had not left a single sermon;
   Attornies-General, awful to the sight,
As hinting more (unless our judgments warp us)
Of the 'Star Chamber' than of 'Habeas Corpus.'

Generals, some all in armour, of the old
   And iron time, ere Lead had ta'en the lead;
Others in wigs of Marlborough's martial fold,
   Huger than twelve of our degenerate breed:
Lordlings with staves of white, or keys of gold:
   Nimrods, whose canvas scarce contain'd the
     steed;
And here and there some stern high Patriot stood,
Who could not get the place for which he sued.

On This Day I Complete My Thirty-Sixth Year

'Tis time this heart should be unmoved,
    Since others it hath ceased to move:
Yet though I cannot be beloved,
                Still let me love!

My days are in the yellow leaf;
    The flowers and fruits of Love are gone;
The worm – the canker, and the grief
                Are mine alone!

The fire that on my bosom preys
    Is lone as some Volcanic Isle;
No torch is kindled at its blaze
                A funeral pile!

The hope, the fear, the jealous care,
    The exalted portion of the pain
And power of Love I cannot share,
                But wear the chain.

But 'tis not *thus* – and 'tis not *here*
    Such thoughts should shake my Soul, nor *now*
Where Glory decks the hero's bier
                Or binds his brow.

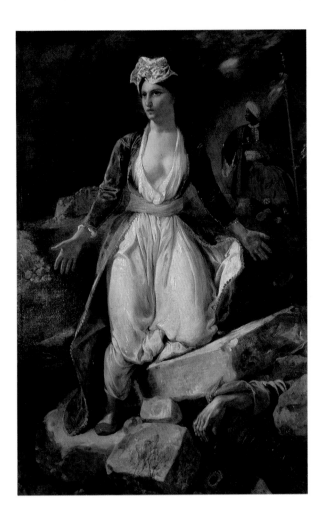

The Sword, the Banner, and the Field,
   Glory and Greece around us see!
The Spartan borne upon his shield
             Was not more free!

Awake (not Greece – she *is* awake!)
   Awake, my Spirit! think through *whom*
Thy life-blood tracks its parent lake
             And then strike home!

Tread those reviving passions down
   Unworthy Manhood – unto thee
Indifferent should the smile or frown
             Of Beauty be.

If thou regret'st thy Youth, *why live?*
   The land of honourable Death
Is here: – up to the Field, and give
             Away thy Breath!

Seek out – less often sought than found –
   A Soldier's Grave, for thee the best;
Then look around, and choose thy Ground,
             And take thy Rest!

SOURCES OF THE EXTRACTS

'Harold in Greece': *Childe Harold's Pilgrimage*, Canto 2, stanzas 85 to 88.

'Harold's Lyric by the Rhine': *Childe Harold*, Canto 3.

'Harold Alone': *Childe Harold*, Canto 3, stanzas 113 to 114.

'Harold in Venice': *Childe Harold*, Canto 4, stanzas 1 to 4, 13, 15.

'Harold's Philosophy': *Childe Harold*, Canto 4, stanzas 136 to 138. ·

'Here in this grotto . . . ': *The Island*, Canto 2, section 15.

'On King George the Third': *The Vision of Judgment*, stanzas 7 to 10.

'On Robert Southey': *The Vision of Judgment*, stanzas 96 to 98.

'On Italy and England': *Beppo*, stanzas 41, 44 to 45, 47 to 49.

'Comparative Morality': *Don Juan*, Canto 1, stanzas 63 to 64.

'First Love': *Don Juan*, Canto 1, stanzas 126 to 127.

'Poetical Commandments': *Don Juan*, Canto 1, stanzas 204 to 205.

'Haidée's Island and a Hangover': *Don Juan*, Canto 2, stanzas 177 to 178.

'Juan and Haidée in Love': *Don Juan*, Canto 2, stanzas 185 to 186, 188 to 189, 192, 194.

'Haidée's Death': *Don Juan*, Canto 4, stanzas 71 to 72.

'The Taking of Ismail and the Horrors of War': *Don Juan*, Canto 8, stanzas 122 to 124.

'The Duke of Wellington': *Don Juan*, Canto 9, stanzas 1 to 6.

'The Prospect of London': *Don Juan*, Canto 10, stanzas 82 to 83.

'Juan on Shooter's Hill': *Don Juan*, Canto 11, stanzas 8 to 13.

'Newstead Abbey Recalled': *Don Juan*, Canto 13, stanzas 66 to 70.

NOTES ON THE PICTURES

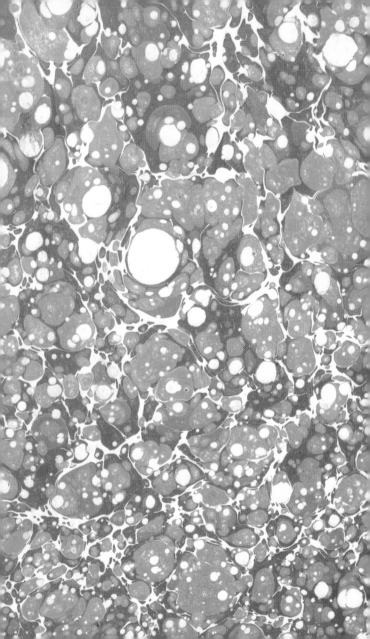